# Indoor Gardening

◄─ A FIRST BOOK ─►

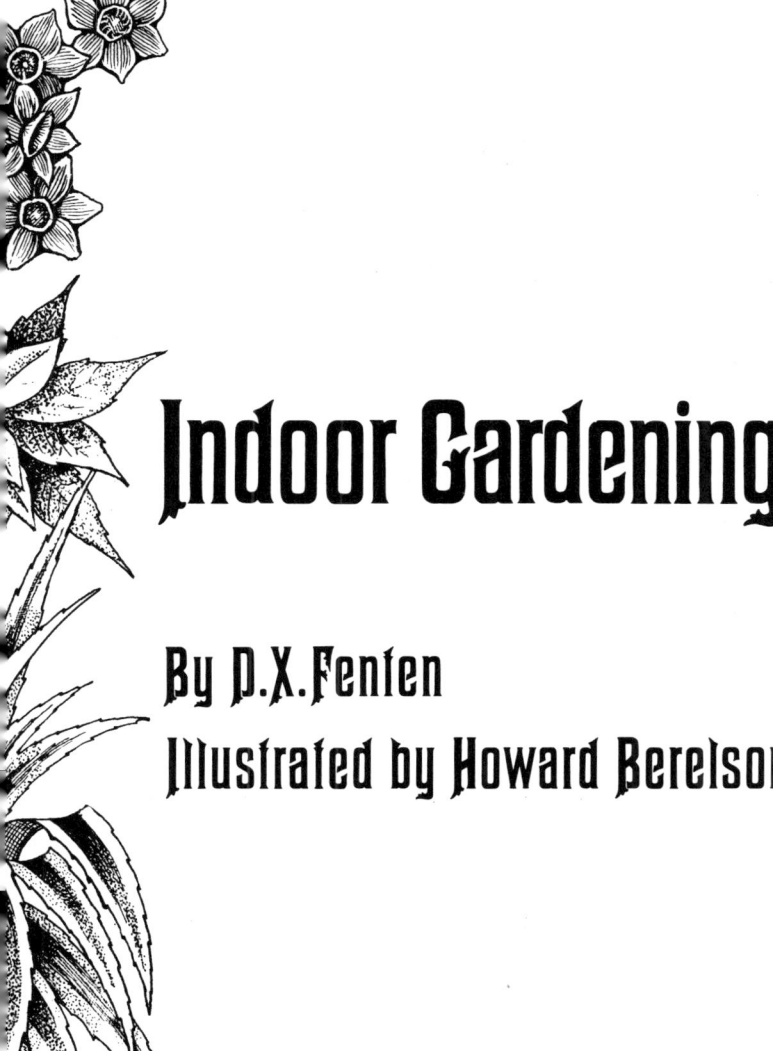

# Indoor Gardening

By D.X. Fenten

Illustrated by Howard Berelson

*Franklin Watts, Inc./New York/1974*

Library of Congress Cataloging in Publication Data
Fenten, D   X
    Indoor gardening.
    (A First book)
    SUMMARY: Instructions on successfully growing such indoor plants as the hibiscus, orchid, passion flower, African violet, and velvet plant.
    1. House plants—Juvenile literature. [1. House plants. 2. Gardening] I. Title.
SB419.F43    635.9'65    74-3278
ISBN 0-531-02731-7
ISBN 0-531-02359-1 (pbk.)

Text copyright © 1974 by D. X. Fenten
Illustrations copyright © 1974 by Franklin Watts, Inc.
Printed in the United States of America
6 5 4 3 2 1

# Contents

Growing Plants Indoors  1
    *Light*  2
    *Water*  4
    *Humidity*  5
    *Ventilation*  5
    *Temperature*  6
    *Soil*  7
    *Fertilizer*  7
    *Containers*  8

Flowers You Grow Indoors  9

All Kinds of Leaves  22

Growing Food Indoors  31

Tiny, Tinier, Tiniest  35

Bulbs for Indoor Bloom   40

Cacti and Succulents   45

Gift Plants   50

Indoor Garden Pests   55

Other Books to Read   57

Index   58

# Indoor Gardening

# Growing Plants Indoors

Although plants were meant to grow outdoors, people liked the way they looked so much that they brought them inside so they could look at them in their homes, their offices, their schools, and their places of worship. When people did that they had to learn a whole new way of taking care of these plants. No longer were their plants growing where nature intended. Now they were growing where people intended.

Growing indoors, the plants were in an environment not meant for growing plants. In some places there was not enough light. In other places the light was not the right kind. In some places it was too hot, in other places it was too cold, too wet, or too dry. But through the years we have worked and learned until today there are thousands of plants that will grow very well indoors, that is, if we give them some special care and attention.

Does this mean that only certain people, those with "green thumbs," can have beautiful, healthy plants indoors? Not at all. Everyone can grow houseplants. Old and young, rich and poor all grow houseplants. They grow them everyplace you could imagine. In cot-

tages, apartments, skyscrapers, on farms, in cities, even on board ships.

People grow houseplants because they want to have something green, something natural, something living, something growing, something beautiful, something real wherever they spend a lot of time.

Houseplants are divided into groups and we can choose from among those that are mainly leafy, those that have beautiful flowers, or even those that have fruits or berries.

Growing plants indoors is simple, inexpensive, challenging, very rewarding, and perhaps most important of all, a lot of fun. You don't need a green thumb, a lot of space, or a large bank account. You don't need a certain kind of pot, expensive "store bought" equipment, or large amounts of botanical knowledge and ability. You do need some information about the plants you want to grow — where they come from and what conditions they like and dislike. You also need the patience to wait days and days and days before "anything happens." And you must like your plants enough to take care of them each and every day.

Is there any deep dark secret to growing plants indoors? Not really, but you must know the "ground" rules. You must know your home and know your plants. You must select plants that will do well in your home, for you cannot expect to make drastic changes in your home to suit your plants. Your plants must suit the house to which you bring them to live.

Let's take a look at the seven keys to good indoor gardening that will open your door to healthy, beautiful, colorful houseplants.

## *Light*

All plants need light to live and to grow. Without light, plants (green ones, not fungi, like mushrooms) cannot make food in their leaves. Some of the food is used to make new leaves, some is used to make flowers, some is used for roots and stems, and much of it is used to keep the plant alive and growing. So, without light to make food, plants soon die.

Not all plants need the same amount and kind of light. Usually plants grown for flowers require more light than plants grown for their leaves. Flowering houseplants need more direct sunlight for longer periods of time than leafy plants do. Houseplants are usually divided into three groups according to the kind of light they need.

*Plants need both light and ventilation, and love a daily misting from a spray bottle filled with water. On the windowsill are a passionflower vine (left) and a geranium.*

Direct sun plants need the brightest sunlight possible for several hours each day. Plants like geraniums and passion flowers do best when they are in full sunlight for many hours each day. If they do not get it their leaves are small, stems are thin, and there are few flowers if any. These plants do best in south windows, but will do well in east or west windows that get plenty of direct sun.

Partial shade plants, including African violets, fuchsia, and gloxinia, like a few hours of direct sunlight each day, but they do best in bright shade. Keep them in east or west windows.

Shade loving plants are mostly leafy plants. They do best with very little direct sun and a lot of bright, sunless shade. Keep them in north windows.

Also remember that the number of hours of light a plant gets has an effect on the amount of food made by the plant. In some plants the number of hours of light controls the time of year the plant blooms. It is very important that you find out the amount and kind of light your plants need if you are to have healthy, pretty houseplants.

## *Water*

Without this important ingredient too, your plants will wither and die. Some will die faster than others, but all plants need water so they can live and grow. Water your plants when they need water, not when your calendar says to "water plants." Look at your plants and their soil every day. Touch the soil. If it is slightly dry, it is time to water. Very few plants need to be dried out completely between waterings.

When you water your plants, give them enough water, but do not drown them. If you are putting the water directly on the soil, pour slowly and steadily until the excess water comes out the drainage hole in the bottom of the flower pot or container. Let the pot stand in the saucer for thirty minutes, pour out any water still in the saucer, and replace the pot.

If you are bottom watering (pouring water into the saucer), the same rule applies. Let the pot sit in the water-filled saucer for thirty minutes then pour out the water. Don't water again until the soil feels dry.

Always try to use water that is at room temperature. If it is too hot or too cold it will shock your plants. And remember, never let plants stand overnight in a saucer full of water. Just like people, plants will get sick if they spend the night with wet feet.

*Humidity*

Another part of the moisture story is humidity. Many houseplants are accustomed to living in areas where there is a lot more moisture in the air than there is in your home. Learn the amount of humidity a plant needs before you buy it. If your house is too dry for a certain plant, buy another kind. If you already own plants that need extra humidity, try placing the plants in a pan that holds an inch of pebbles or sand. Keep the pebbles or sand moist at all times, but never let the water level get high enough to touch the bottom of your pots. It is also helpful to "mist" your plants or spray them gently with water.

*Ventilation*

The air in your house is very important to your plants in two other ways. All plants need some fresh air if they are to grow well, but they don't like drafts or strong breezes. Open the windows at least once a day (even during winter months) to let in fresh air, but make sure that the plants are not in the same rooms as the open windows. This way fresh air will come in but your plants will not be harmed by cold air or drafts.

A great many houseplants are very sensitive to gas. Some will not bloom and others will drop leaves or turn yellow at the faintest hint of gas. The plants will react to the gas long before you can smell it. Changing the air in a room at least once a day will avoid any problems caused by gas from your kitchen stove or heating system.

*Houseplants need humidity and setting the pots in pans filled with moist pebbles is a good way to create it. From left: African violet and fuschia.*

## Temperature

Most houseplants will do well at the same temperatures preferred by humans. But there are some that will not grow well at temperatures that are either too high or too low. It is important that these plants be kept at the temperatures they require if you want them to do as well as they can.

Just about all houseplants do best when the nighttime temperatures are 10° to 15° lower than the daytime temperatures. Put plants into a cooler room at night and you will have healthier plants with better color. Never keep plants on windowsills when nights are cold. Either move them back from the window or put a newspaper or other material between the plant and the window.

*Soil*

Most houseplants grow well in a "regular" houseplant mix, while the remainder do exceptionally well when variations are made. Only a few things are musts — the soil must drain well, hold some moisture and nutrients, and allow some air to get to the roots.

Every garden shop and plant nursery and most variety stores have a houseplant soil mixture for sale. These are excellent, clean, and easy to use. But if you want to mix your own, try these combinations:

Flowering plants — equal parts of potting soil, coarse sand, and peat moss.

Foliage plants — equal parts of potting soil and peat moss, small amount of coarse sand.

Cacti and similar plants — equal parts of potting soil and peat moss, double the amount of coarse sand.

*Fertilizer*

Few houseplants die from lack of food, but many die of indigestion. Don't overfeed your houseplants. If you have the feeling that when a little is good then a lot is better . . . don't.

Feed your plants only during the time that they are really growing. When they are resting or only growing a little bit, usually in the winter when there is less light, leave them alone.

The best and safest fertilizers to use on your houseplants are labeled organic and water soluble. Just dissolve the liquid or powder in water and pour this into the soil at the same time you are watering. Read the label on the package or jar very carefully and only use as much fertilizer as the manufacturer suggests. Don't add any more "for good measure."

*Containers*

Now that you have all the other ingredients for good indoor gardening, you need one thing more — pots to put your plants into. You can use almost anything that will hold both soil and water. Every garden shop has all sorts of pots from which to choose — clay, plastic, metal, fiberboard, and many, many more. You can select from among these, or you can make your own from objects you have around the house. If you look around you will find many containers — polyfoam or plastic; plastic detergent or bleach bottle halves; a pretty cup or china soup bowl; or anything else that will hold soil and water.

Whichever type of pot you choose, bought or "homemade," check on a few things before you start your planting. For example, does your pot have a drainage hole? These holes in the bottom of pots allow the excess water to get out and keep your plant from drowning or sitting for long periods of time with wet feet. If your container doesn't have a drainage hole, make a layer of broken clay pot pieces or pebbles or gravel in the bottom of the pot.

Is your pot going to be big enough for your plant when it is full grown? If you use a pot that is big enough for your plant today, it will probably be much too small once the plant starts to grow. You can either expect to move your plants from small pots into larger ones or you can buy large enough ones at the start. Usually, however, a plant is most comfortable in a pot its own size.

# Flowers You Grow Indoors

Everyone loves flowers. That's why we give them as gifts, send them on occasions to show that we remember, wear them at parties and special events, and grow them inside and outside the places we live and work.

Many people think flowers are much more difficult to grow indoors than any other kinds of plants. This is not true as long as you know your plants and what they need.

Here are some flowering plants you should try. They are easy to grow, will do well in most homes, and are beautiful all the time — in bloom as well as out of bloom. They are listed here alphabetically according to their Latin name or family name, in case nurserymen in your part of the country use different popular names. When the plants have a common name, it's also included.

Check the description of the plants to see if they are what you like and what you want to grow. Then, after choosing, follow the simple suggestions for caring for your plants and your house will soon be full of color, aroma, and beauty.

*Abutilon* (Flowering Maple)

Don't give this plant too much room and you will get many more pretty, paper thin, bell-shaped flowers than you would otherwise. That's right, keep it in a pot that is slightly smaller than what you think the plant needs and you will increase the number of flowers. Abutilon has very pretty green, maplelike leaves to go with the red-yellow, white, yellow, salmon, or purple blossoms. Though these plants can grow to several feet, keep the branches trimmed to a compact eighteen inches. Abutilon is a trailing plant and looks nice in a hanging basket.

Easy to grow, abutilon likes plenty of water, at least four hours of sunlight a day, and fertilizer once a month. Temperatures should be kept at about 70° during the day and 55° at night.

*Aeschynanthus Parvifolus* (Lipstick Plant)

Lipstick plants are also called basket vines because they look best in hanging baskets. Natives of Java, these plants bloom in the spring and produce buds that look like lipsticks on stems. The stems can grow up to four feet long, so there are many "lipsticks" on each stem. There are many different varieties so you can pick scarlet, orange, or yellow "lipsticks."

They are not as pleased with strong sunlight as some plants. Lipstick plants grow and bloom beautifully with about four hours of daily bright shade or sunlight filtered through a gauzy curtain. Add extra peat moss to the potting soil mixture and supply plenty of water. Lipstick plants come from a warm climate so keep your house at about 65° during the evening and raise it to at least 75° during the day. Fertilize once a month.

*Azalea*

Usually thought of as outdoor shrubs, azaleas can be grown indoors. When they bloom (in the spring), the entire plant is covered with flowers. Different varieties have red, pink, white, or a combination of colors. When the flowers disappear the plant is still lovely to look at because it has very pretty dark green leaves. This plant grows to two feet in height.

Azaleas do best when potted in a regular potting mixture that has a double portion of peat moss. They like as much early morning or late afternoon sunlight as they can get, with at least four hours a day minimum in an east or west window. Temperature is also very important. Keep azaleas at about 68° during the day and about 50° at night, and protect them from drafts. Water thoroughly. Fertilize with acid-heavy fertilizer every two weeks *only* between the time the flowers fade in spring and new buds form in summer. Do not fertilize at any other time.

## *Begonia*

There are more different kinds of begonias for growing indoors than any other kind of plant, so you must try some of these. Wax begonias have many small (about one inch across) flowers in pink, red, or white that grow in front of waxy leaves that are green or red-green. Many varieties have leaves that grow to four inches across and the plants bloom all year long. Rex begonias have small white or pink hanging flowers. They are best known for their hairy, handsome leaves shaped like an elephant's ears, which grow very large and come in combinations of green, red, bronze, and red-green.

Wax begonias thrive in direct sunlight; Rex begonias must be kept out of direct sunlight. All do best with cool night temperatures (about 55°) and warm day temperatures (about 70°). Water well but allow to dry out before watering again. Feed every two weeks when growing. To keep begonias blooming, remove all dead flowers regularly. Wax begonias also can get "leggy," or overgrown, and benefit from being cut back.

### *Beloperone* (Shrimp Plant)

Another all-year-bloomer, the shrimp plant got its name from its hanging white flowers growing out of reddish bracts. Glance at them and they look like shrimp. Varieties come in yellow, red, and red and yellow. Hairy, pea-green leaves sometimes grow as long as the hanging bracts.

Shrimp plants come from Mexico and prefer warm temperatures during the day (about 70°) and four to five hours of bright sunlight. At night they like cooler temperatures — no higher than 55°. Use a regular potting mixture and don't overwater. In fact, allow the soil to become a bit dry between waterings. Because the plant tends to get scraggly, pinch off the ends when the branches are twelve to eighteen inches long and keep the plant to this size. For all year blooming, fertilize every two weeks.

### *Bougainvillea* (Paper-flower)

You can decide exactly how large you want these tropical American vines to grow in your home. Choose a height from two to fifteen feet and keep the plant cut back to that size. You'll not only get a fast-growing, pretty, treelike plant, but one with lots of color. Bracts (leaf parts found near the base of the flower) are more colorful than the flowers themselves and come in red, pink, purple, copper, and white.

Bougainvilleas like warm weather so keep temperatures in the upper 60°s and low 70°s. Be sure the soil mixture is equal parts of humus, sand, potting soil, and peat moss and is kept very moist during the summer, almost dry during the winter. Plants will bloom in spring and summer and rest during fall and winter. Feed every other week during the blooming season, not at all during the resting period.

### *Calceolaria* (Pocketbook Plant)

Though they only last a year and flower only once during that time, these wonderful little plants are worth growing because of their unusual flowers. Also called pouch flower, calceolaria has numbers of puffed-up blossom pouches growing above large green leaves. The flowers grow in two parts, with the top lip much less puffy than the lower lip. They come in many different colors, but most are either a shade of red or of yellow with a variety of spots, stripes, and other markings.

A little more difficult to grow than other plants, calceolaria likes an even day temperature (around 60°) when young and growing. Night temperatures should be on the cool side (45°). Water when soil becomes dry and keep in a spot that gets plenty of fresh air. Do not fertilize the plant when flowers appear.

*Crossandra*

Not too many houseplants will bloom throughout the year. Grow crossandra properly and you will have salmon-orange colored flowers to enjoy in every season. Full-grown plants are about one to two feet tall and are covered with dark green leaves. This plant, a native of the East Indies, is started from seed and blooms about nine months after planting.

Crossandras like the early morning sun in the east windows of your home and warm temperatures all day. They need a temperature of about 70° day and night. Pot the plants in a mixture of one part potting soil, one part sand, one part humus, and two parts peat moss. Keep the soil nice and moist, mist the plant frequently, and add plant food every other week.

*Cyclamen* (Shooting Star)

Cyclamen is a native of the Mediterranean and one of the prettiest houseplants. It has large, showy, red, white, or pink flowers on the end of slender stems. Its thick, green, heart-shaped leaves are marked in silver or white and form a beautiful background for the two- to three-inch flowers. It blooms from November to April.

*Cyclamens are among the prettiest of gift plants but require quite cool temperatures.*

Cyclamen have to have quite cool temperatures no higher than 60° during the day and 50°-55° at night. To raise them yourself, pot the cyclamen in a soil mixture of equal parts peat moss, potting soil, humus, and sand. Soil should be moist, but not soggy; do not pour the water on the plant itself, but water from the side of the pot. Feed twice a month and keep the budding plants in some, but not too much, sunlight.

Once the flowering stops and the leaves start to die, put the tuber into cool storage. Pick it out of the soil, shake off any potting mixture, and put it into a cool, dark place. In the fall repot so that about half of the tuber is above the soil, water, give bright light, and start all over again.

## *Fuchsia* (Lady's Eardrops)

Trailing or upright, there are few plants as pretty as fuchsia in bloom. The flowers are crimson, pink, white, or a combination of these colors, and look like fat, round bells or old-fashioned full skirts. Most of these plants bloom only in spring and summer, but you can get them to bloom over more of the year with extra special care and treatment. Upright plants grow to about three feet tall and the trailing variety grow and grow.

Though fuchsias like sun, they don't like direct sunlight, so be sure they are protected. Keep moist while they are growing and feed every two weeks. Less water and less food are necessary when they are dormant (sleeping). Prune (cut back) both before each blooming season and while the plant is growing so that it takes on a bushier, fuller look.

## *Gloxinia*

These velvet-flowered Brazilian beauties grow from tubers at various times during the year. The bell-shaped flowers come in white, pink, red, purple, various shades of each, and sometimes with contrasting spots and edges. Once you have seen these magnificent blooms, you will never forget them.

Gloxinias like lots and lots of light each day (but direct sunlight will shrivel the leaves) and warm day and night temperatures. Pot the tubers in a mixture that contains extra peat moss, water thoroughly and regularly, and feed once a month. After blooming, remove tubers, keep them in a cool spot, let them rest for two or three months, then repot and you are ready for truly beautiful flowers again.

## *Hibiscus* (Rose-of-China)

Easy to grow, beautiful, and extremely long lived are all descriptions of the wonderful Chinese hibiscus. The plants bloom all year round, and, with proper care, can do this for at least twenty-five years. The five-inch wide papery blossoms come in shades of white, cream, yellow, pink, salmon, and red. Though hibiscus grow very tall, they can be kept at four feet with careful pruning. The branches you prune, if they have some "woody" stem, can be easily rooted in damp sand or vermiculite.

Keep your hibiscus in as much sun as possible, give it plenty of water, feed once a month, and enjoy the blooms that open fully all through the year.

*Impatiens* (Patience Plant)

Also called "Patient Lucy," this plant is known for its habit of shooting seeds in all directions as its exploding seed pods become ripe. Easy to grow, impatiens will bloom almost all year long in a sunny window. With many varieties from which to choose, you can get these small plants to grow with white, pink, coral, purple, or bicolor flowers and green, maroon, or white-edged leaves.

*With careful planning, you can have indoor plants blooming during every month of the year. From left:* Paphiopedilum *orchid, hibiscus, episcia, azalea, shrimp plant, and impatiens.*

From East Africa, impatiens like lots and lots of sunlight and lots and lots of water. Pot in a mixture that has extra peat moss and keep in a spot where temperatures stay around 65° to 70°. Fertilize every two weeks and make frequent cuttings for more plants for yourself, to give as gifts, and to keep the plants blooming and bushy.

## *Kalanchoe*

A whole group of plants that bloom in the winter, kalanchoes have fleshy green leaves and clusters of many tiny red, orange, or yellow flowers. Try several different varieties to find your favorite.

Considered to be "short-day" plants, kalanchoes need more time in darkness than in sunlight. Give them at least four hours of bright sunlight each day and then put them into a dark place if you want them to flower. Keep day temperatures warm (72°) and night temperatures cool (55°). Water only when soil is dry to the touch and fertilize every two weeks when plant is flowering.

## *Lantana*

Take your pick — plants that grow upright and have loads of tiny flower clusters, tree-shaped plants that have loads of tiny flower clusters, or plants that trail loads of tiny flower clusters from hanging baskets. That is lantana. You can choose from among such colors as white, pink, yellow, lavender, red, orange, and an assortment of combinations.

For regular upright growth, pinch back stem tips so plant remains a shrubby twelve inches tall. A bit more pruning and you have a handsome, flowering lantana tree. If you prefer trailers, let the plant hang out of a basket until the branches get about four feet long. Give all lantanas good, direct sunlight — at least five hours each day. Water when the soil gets dry and feed twice each month. Keep the temperature at about 70° during the day and a bit cooler at night.

*Orchids*

Orchids are a whole family of plants you can grow in your own home. They are often expensive plants; they take a bit of time and trouble, but they're worth the effort. Orchids grow two ways — in soil (terrestrial) or on trees (epiphytic). Pot terrestrial orchids just as you would any other plants. To pot epiphytic orchids, use shredded bark or osmunda fiber. If you can keep the moisture content of your home up by using a humidifier or other device, you can grow magnificent orchid flowers. Each orchid has its own requirements, likes, and dislikes, so read about them before you buy them. Usually a home where the temperature stays between 66° and 72° is fine for orchids. Water well while they are blooming and feed well during the flower season. Then give them a rest before they are to bloom again.

Some varieties to try include Acinetta, Brassavola, Cattleya, Cycnoches, Epidendrum, Odontoglossum, Oncidium, Paphiopedilum, Phalaenopsis, Stanhopea, and Vanda.

*Passiflora* (Passionflower)

The flowers on these Brazilian beauties must be seen to be believed. Growing on a vine, the intricate blossoms reach a size of four to five inches across and come in white, pink, purple, and combinations of each. The vines can grow to six feet tall, so give them plenty of room. Pot in a tub large enough for their spreading roots.

Not too picky about its growing conditions, passionflower does best on about five hours of direct sun every day and a lot of water. Pot in regular potting soil mixture and keep temperatures at about 65° day and night (except in winter when the vine should rest at 55°). Fertilize it every two weeks during its growing season.

*Pelargonium* (Geranium)

There are hundreds of different kinds of geraniums available so pick and choose exactly the kind you like. There are the familiar, old-fashioned kind called *zonals* (because of the "zone" of brown-green on the leaves) and the newer fancy-leaf geraniums (zonals with various color combinations and tones). Martha Washingtons have beautifully veined leaves and bloom in the spring with flowers that are blends of two or three colors. Ivy-leaved types are perfect for hanging baskets and scented-leaved geraniums have handsome, pleasant smelling leaves. There are also dwarf types that have pretty blooms all through the year. Last on the list are the carefree types that can be grown from seed into bushy little plants covered with flowers.

Though each type of geranium differs from the others, all like cool temperatures, small pots, and potting mixtures that are heavy on the soil and light on the peat moss. Don't overwater or overfeed and give them even less water and food when they have finished blooming. They will not bloom unless they have lots and lots of direct sunlight.

*Saintpaulia* (African Violet)

Many people feel that African violets are what indoor gardening is all about. Thousands of varieties are available, and many of them are quite inexpensive. Try three or four and then decide on your own favorites. There are pink, white, blue, purple, and combination colors, with single and double flowers, as well as ruffled. If you follow a few simple suggestions, you can get them to bloom all year long.

African violets like light, but not direct sunlight. Keep them out of the sun but give them plenty of bright light (such as behind the window curtains). They should be located in north, east, or west windows. Pot them in a mixture that has extra peat moss added to a "regular" potting soil mixture. You can also buy special African violet soil in bags. Do not water too much — water sparingly and never get it on the leaves. If water gets on the leaves it will spot them and spoil their looks. African violets are good plants to water from the bottom. Keep your plants in places where the temperature is always about 70°. Fertilize once a month.

### *Senecio* (Mexican Flame Vine)

This plant and all its sisters are worth growing because of their colorful flowers. Mexican flame vine bears deep orange daisylike flowers several times during the year. The flowers are about one and one-half inches across. A sister plant, called parlor ivy, has tiny yellow flowers that measure only about one-half inch across but are formed into pretty two-to-three-inch clusters.

Another sister, cineraria, is also beautiful, with large clusters of deeply colored, velvet-looking, daisylike flowers. The flowers are either red, blue, purple, or pink and white with white centers for some. Its large leaves are green on top and purple green underneath. Cineraria flowers can be four inches across.

All of this family like about four hours of sunlight during the summer months and whatever they can get at other times of the year. Cinerarias like slightly cooler temperatures than the others in the family (50° at night, 65° in the daytime) and lots of moisture. Mexican flame vine and parlor ivy like 55° temperatures at night and about 70° during the day. They also like frequent watering and fertilizer every other week.

# All Kinds of Leaves

Solid colors. Striped. Spotted. Banded. Spear shaped. Ruffled. Long thin ones. Short fat ones. All kinds of leaves. Foliage plants are plants whose leaves are much prettier than their flowers. And the selection of foliage plants increases every year.

Usually a bit easier to grow in the home than some flowering plants, many foliage plants will grow well even if neglected for long periods of time. Others will continue to do well even under very poor growing conditions. In most cases, foliage plants either will not bloom indoors or have very plain or unattractive flowers. However, they more than make up for this with their beautiful and often unusual leaves.

Choose from among an almost unending collection of colors, sizes, and shapes. Choose them for a particular place in your home or school. Choose them because you like to look at and grow beautiful plants. Here are some that you can try. They are all easy to grow and are especially pretty. Try some of them, then try some more. You will find many at your local nursery or garden shop, or you can order them by mail from flower and seed catalogs.

*Aglaonema* (Chinese Evergreen)

It is almost impossible accidentally to kill these pretty green-leafed plants, so perhaps they are the best kind for the beginner. They are natives of the far east and the most popular variety is the one with the pointed, solid green leaf.

Give this plant even moisture and a little light and you might even get a very pretty white flower. Pot in a mixture that has extra peat moss and you will have a lot of leaves. Try growing it in water — no soil — and you will be surprised at how well it does. Add a piece of aquarium charcoal to the water to keep it sweet.

*Araucaria* (Norfolk Island Pine)

A real pine, this small tree can grow to about two hundred feet in its home on Norfolk Island, New Zealand. Indoors, three to five feet is just about right. Get one of these and start it growing early in the year and you will have a beautiful, tiny, live Christmas tree when the time comes.

Keep these trees in cool places, especially during the wintertime, and never in temperatures over 70°. Pot in regular potting soil that is kept moist and give plenty of light. Too little light and the plant loses its beautiful, even shape.

*Aspidistra* (Cast-Iron Plant)

This plant was named by someone who had a sense of humor and wanted to tell us that it would grow under all sorts of poor conditions. For example, the cast-iron plant will do well even if the temperature is too high, the air is too dry, and the light is very poor. One variety has two to two-and-a-half foot shiny, arching, almost black-green leaves. Other varieties have green and white striped leaves and white spotted leaves.

When it has a choice, aspidistra grows best in light shade and daytime temperatures of 70°. At night, this plant from China prefers cool temperatures, around 50°. Keep it potted in a regular potting soil mixture that is kept moist at all times.

## Bromeliads

How about trying some plants from the same family as the pineapple? Bromeliads are the same family as the pineapple, and if you have had trouble growing other plants, you will not have trouble with these. There are a great many different varieties, many of which have leaves that look a lot like the sansevieria (see page 30). You can get varieties whose leaves are green, pink, purple, white, or all sorts of combinations including spots, stripes, dots, and dashes.

Just about all the members of this family like to sit in the sun in soil that is regular except for a bit of extra sand. Water a lot during warm weather, filling the cup the whorl of leaves makes, but give a lot less during the cold months; then water only when soil has become quite dry. It's a good idea to let tap water stand a day before using on bromeliads. They are sensitive to chlorine and this way it can escape.

## Calathea

A member of the same family as the maranta (prayer plant), these tropical plants from Brazil grow a great number of pretty leaves quickly. The leaves are marked on top or underneath with gray-green, purple, or dark green.

These plants do not like too much sun so keep them in a spot that is light but shaded. Pot in a regular potting soil mixture that is kept moist. Temperatures during daytime hours should be no lower than 70°. Feed twice a month with an organic, water soluble plant food.

*Foliage plants are among the most successful indoor plants and will often grow well even if neglected. Clockwise from the top: cast-iron plant, dumb cane, snake plant, calathea, peperomia, velvet plant, philodendron, Chinese evergreen, coleus, and in the center, a bromeliad.*

## *Coleus*

These foliage plants from Java come in more colors and more combinations of colors than you can imagine. Some include scarlet, maroon, red, yellow, pink, and many, many quite different shades of green. Coleus grows about twelve to eighteen inches tall without too much help from you.

Pot in regular potting soil, keep moist, and give a good deal of sunlight or brightness. It has tiny blue flowers that should be pinched off so more pretty leaves will grow.

## *Croton*

These plants, from the tropical Malayan area, come in so many sizes, colors, and shapes, it is impossible to see or try them all. Not only are varieties different, but no two plants within a variety are the same; often leaves on the same plant have different colors and patterns. Some leaves are flat and oval, others are twisted like a corkscrew. Leaves are green (all shades) and splotched, spotted, striped, and veined with yellows, reds, oranges, browns, and pinks.

Give these plants good light but not much direct sunlight. A bright window that gets no direct sunlight is best. Be sure crotons are in regular potting soil mix that has a bit more sand added for drainage. If these plants sit in water they yellow and die. They like warm (70°) temperatures with high humidity during the day and even watering, but not a drowning.

## *Dieffenbachia* (Dumb Cane)

These plants can leave you speechless — not from their beauty, but from their sap! If the sap gets into your mouth it causes the tongue to swell, which will stop you from eating or speaking, hence the name "dumb cane." These are big, beautiful plants with stripes, spots, and blotches of white and ivory.

Dumb canes are very easy to grow in any home. Pot them in a regular potting mixture, and keep them in a light area but out of direct sunlight. Water only after the soil has become quite dry.

## *Dracaena*

Because its long leaves look a bit like corn-stalk leaves, this African native is sometimes called the corn plant. But that is its only similarity to corn. The two most popular dracaena have long, tapered, sword-shaped leaves; one with wide yellow bands down the middle of the green and the other with white-green bands on the edges of the leaves. Both are very pretty, and quick growing.

To get the longest, prettiest leaves, give this plant some light but not too much direct sunlight. Pot in a regular mixture that is kept moist but not soaked. After that, just leave it alone and it will grow well, even if conditions are not exactly right.

## *Ficus* (Rubber Plant)

India and Malaya give us these plants with their very large, usually very colorful leaves. Relatives of the fig tree, these decorative house plants can be grown as small plants or can be trained to become large, indoor trees. The best known varieties are called the Indian Rubber Tree (because of the milky white sap that looks like liquid rubber but is not) and the Fiddle Leaf Fig (because its leaves are fiddle shaped).

Pot these varieties in regular potting mixture that you keep moist in spring and summer and allow to dry out a bit in winter. Keep the plants in bright light and wash the leaves frequently with water. *Never* try to polish the leaves with oil or anything else.

## *Gynura* (Velvet Plant)

A hairy, purple plant? That is gynura. The beautiful leaves are completely covered with short, brilliantly colored, purple hair. Set in a sunny window, the entire plant seems to glow. From Java, this plant is outstanding all by itself or as the focal point of a green foliage group or combined with pink flowering begonias.

A sunny window, moisture, regular potting soil, and frequent pruning and you will have a plant that will stop traffic with its beauty. Be sure to pinch back often or the plant will get very stringy and look much less attractive.

*These foliage plants like light, but not direct sunlight. Trailing ivy, graceful-leaved dracaena, and the upright Norfolk Island pine make a handsome combination.*

### *Hedera* (Ivy)

A great many interesting varieties of this "English Ivy" come from Morocco, the Canary Islands, and the Azores. And the leaves come in as many different shapes, colors, and textures as there are varieties of the plant. Some are solid green, in various shades, and some have white and yellow marking. All are worth trying.

Ivy is very easy to grow if you keep the leaves washed with water and the house temperature under 70° in the winter. Pot in regular potting mix that is kept moist. Give as much light as possible, with little direct sunlight.

### *Peperomia*

There are a great many varieties of these pretty foliage plants and they come in a great many colors — gray, white, silver, maroon, brown, and, of course, several shades of green. Most of the peperomia varieties are low, bushy growers so they are excellent houseplants. A few have trailing leaves and these make wonderful hanging basket plants. Try several of these — they are fun to grow and watch.

All peperomia varieties like pretty much the same kind of conditions. Pot them in regular potting mixture and water thoroughly but only when the soil has become quite dry. Keep your plants in a warm spot that gets plenty of light but very little direct sunlight.

### *Philodendron*

There are so many different kinds of philodendron to grow it is impossible not to find at least several that will be your own favorites. There are climbing types, trailing types, solid-leaved and cut-leaved types. There are olive greens, green greens, and black greens. And they are all almost impossible to kill. They will do well whether they are watered or dry, in full sunlight or stuck away in a corner that never sees the sun. You will have to try many of these so you can see for yourself why people think they were created especially for growing indoors under all sorts of conditions.

If you want the best for your philodendrons, pot them in regular potting mixture. Keep the soil moist and give them some light, but not sunlight, from time to time.

### *Sansevieria* (Snake Plant)

Another difficult-to-kill foliage plant comes in two varieties from South Africa and India. The first variety is tall and upright with leaves that are long, tapering, and spearlike. The second is short, squat, and sort of bird's-nest-like. The short kind grows to about eight inches, the tall kind can grow to five feet. Leaves are green, blue-green, dark green, or just green, and are banded or margined with white, cream, or bright yellow.

Keep these plants in a light area of the house, but out of the sunlight. Pot in regular potting soil mixture that you water only when the soil feels dry. Though the plant will live if kept dry, it will only grow if watered. It's helpful to sponge the leaves every so often with water.

# Growing Food Indoors

Can you imagine an orange tree in your bedroom? Or a peach tree in your living room? How about tomatoes or herbs growing in your kitchen? Would you like to grow a lemon the size of a baseball in your classroom?

You can grow all sorts of good things to eat right in your own home. Many of these plants and trees are very easy to grow and ask very little help and attention from you. Here are some you should try as soon as possible. Then, when you see how easy and exciting it is to grow your own fruits and vegetables indoors, you will want to try some more.

Start out with the unbelievable Ponderosa lemon (Citrus limonia). Imagine, a juicy lemon weighing about two pounds that you grew at home, and from a tree that is considered a dwarf tree!

Most of the ground rules you must follow to grow these giant lemons also apply to such other citrus fruits as the Calamondin orange (Citrus mitis), the Otaheite orange (Citrus taitensis), and several others. So when you learn the rules for one, you learn them for all.

Just about all the citrus plants can be started from the seeds of the fruit, but this is not a good idea if you want fruit while you are still young. Dwarf citrus need at least seven years of growth before they can start fruiting. Buy a dwarf citrus plant from a nurseryman and you will get action much sooner.

When you bring your plant home, pot it in a large pot, barrel, bucket, or planter filled with a regular potting mixture that has extra amounts of peat moss and sand added. Be certain the pot you choose is large enough for the tree when it is fully grown. Most dwarf citrus

trees grow to about two feet in height and two feet in diameter. Also be certain the pot you choose has a drainage hole in the bottom. These fruit trees like moisture, but they will not do well if they are allowed to stand in soggy soil.

Give your trees plenty of sunlight, fresh air, and warm temperatures — about 55° at night and about 70° or above during the day.

When all of this is done, you must give nature some help. Out-of-doors bees and insects move in and out of the flowers on fruit trees spreading pollen from one flower to the next. Indoors, you must do the job of pollination.

When the flowers on your dwarf fruit tree are very large and very open, get to work. With a brand new artist's paintbrush, take

*Fruits and vegetables can be grown indoors. These citrus trees, Calamondin orange (left) and Ponderosa lemon, must be hand pollinated to bear fruit, as should the Tiny Tim tomato plant. The little pot is filled with the herb chives.*

the pollen (it looks like fine dust) from the inside of one flower and carefully spread it around the inside of another flower. Do not touch the pollen or the bristles of the brush with your fingers. Go gently and carefully from flower to flower, until you have pollinated all the flowers. Then you will almost certainly start to see fruit begin to form in less than one week.

Other dwarf trees you should try are the Persian lime, Nagami kumquat, pomegranate, and plum. If you have a little more room and larger tubs, try growing dwarf peaches and pears indoors. You can do it and have fun watching and waiting to harvest your full-sized, delicious fruit from these little trees.

There are many more good things to eat that you can grow indoors. For example, you can grow vegetables and herbs right in the kitchen. Choose from among the dwarf varieties of these plants, give them plenty of sunlight, just the right amount of water, and regular fertilizer feedings. Because your plants are young and delicate, feed with a weak mixture of water soluble fertilizer. You can make a weak mixture by using only half the amount of fertilizer suggested on the label to the full amount of water.

Vegetables like tomatoes, peppers, beans, and eggplants need your help for pollination. Others like onions, lettuce, most salad greens, and herbs will grow beautifully indoors without your help as a substitute bee.

You can choose from the dwarf varieties of vegetables including Pixie, Tiny Tim, and Patio tomatoes, Little Leaguer cabbage, Golden or White Midget corn, Tiny Sweet or Short'n Sweet carrots, and Tom Thumb lettuce. A whole pan of different kinds of herbs takes up very little space. You can order these dwarf seeds from any seed catalog or find them in your local nursery store.

Indoor gardening can include many good things to eat as long as the plants are small but the amount of care and attention is large. You must keep watching your dwarf trees and vegetables, but it is well worth it.

# Tiny, Tinier, Tiniest

We've just finished talking about dwarf varieties and though they are smaller than normal varieties, they are not nearly the smallest plants you can grow indoors. If you would like to try some really tiny, really beautiful plants, try the miniatures.

In the plant world, dwarf plants are smaller than regular-sized plants. Some dwarfs of very large trees or shrubs can grow several feet tall. Miniatures are the smallest plants there are — all of them are quite a bit smaller than the dwarf varieties. Some miniatures, when full grown, are no more than a few inches tall.

The same rules apply to miniature plants grown indoors as apply to the larger varieties of the same plant. That is, if regular African violets like brightness and no direct sunlight, a potting mixture with extra peat moss and watering only from the bottom, give the same treatment to miniature African violets.

You can use miniature flowering plants and foliage plants the same way you use regular plants. Put them in pots, window boxes, hanging baskets, and everywhere you want tiny, beautiful plants.

*Miniature roses blooming in a tea cup turned into a flower pot.*

But if you want something special from tiny plants, plant them in dish gardens and terrariums. A dish garden is a group of small plants arranged in a dish or in another container, like a teacup, glass jar, or soup bowl. There are no tops on these containers and air can move freely around the plants and the soil. Terrariums are small gardens that are completely enclosed in glass. Containers or terrariums include drinking glasses, old jars, glass domes, and even fish bowls. The real difference between terrariums and dish gardens is that a terrarium has a cover and a dish garden doesn't.

Though you can make any arrangement you like, dish garden and terrarium plants are usually arranged so they look like scenes from nature. Before you actually do anything with the plants, do something about your container. To make a beautiful, inexpensive terrarium garden, choose a container from the many you are certain to have around your house. Look for quart size and larger mayonnaise jars, old, out-of-use fish bowls or aquariums, preserving or jelly jars, candy jars or any other glass or clear plastic containers. Be certain the container you choose either has a cover or at least can be closed by laying a piece of glass over the opening. One of the features of a terrarium is that it rarely, if ever, needs watering after the first time. The cover or glass top keeps moisture in the container where it collects on the sides, runs down, and waters the soil. This will happen continuously, without your help — if you set up your garden under glass correctly.

Whichever kind of container you choose, wash it carefully and completely, inside and out. If you use anything other than water to do the cleaning, let the container stand for a day or two after the

*Terrariums are the perfect way to grow and show off your miniature or dwarf plants, and you can choose almost any type of plant from cacti to moisture-loving tropicals.*

washing session. Strong fumes from cleaning liquids can harm delicate plants. If you allow the container to "air out," the fumes will go off into the air.

Your next step is to get some moss. If you live near a wooded area you may find some growing at the base of a large tree. If you can't find any, buy some from your local flower shop. Line the bottom and lower sides of the container with the moss, green side facing out. When your scene has been completed, the moss will look a lot nicer than just plain soil. Once the moss is in place, start adding some pebbles. Add enough pebbles or gravel so there is about one inch of them covering the moss in the bottom of the container.

Charcoal goes into the container next. You can buy this at any pet store. The kind you want is washed and ready to be put into fish tank filters. Put a thin layer of the charcoal on top of the pebbles or gravel. Use a small funnel to aim everything into place in the container, especially the two-inch layer of potting soil that goes on top of the charcoal. If you can get your hand inside the container, use it to form the soil into tiny hills and valleys, just as you have seen in nature. Do not flatten the soil down, as this will make the scene look very fake.

Now you are ready to place your plants. Choose from among the miniature varieties of the plants that "belong" in your scene. For example, use various kinds of miniature cacti for a desert scene or tiny roses for an under-glass miniature flower garden. You can plan and plant a tropical forest, a colorful flower garden, an evergreen mountain, or a dry-as-dust desert.

Though many of the miniature plants can be grown from seed, it is a better idea to buy small plants from a local nurseryman or from a mail order nurseryman. When your plants arrive, tap them carefully out of their pots and place them in holes you've dug in the soil in the container. Press the plants into place either with your fingers or with a long, thin stick, padded on the end to make a good tamper. When all the plants are in place and the scene is as you want it to be, carefully water the plants, put the cover or glass sheet on the container, and place it in a bright but not sunny window.

If you want to try a dish garden instead of a terrarium, follow the same steps. But once your scene is complete, you must watch it and water it as often as necessary. Left to dry out, these tiny plants will soon die. Properly cared for, miniature plants in either dish gardens or terrariums will look like little jewels in your home for many years.

# Bulbs for Indoor Bloom

Can we make flowers bloom indoors during the time they are supposed to be sleeping? Can we force plants to bloom when we want them to instead of letting them bloom at their normal time? Anyone who has ever worked with flower bulbs knows the answer is "Yes" to both of these questions. Gardeners call this process of getting plants to bloom ahead of their normal time "forcing." The secret to successful forcing is to treat the bulbs or plants as close to the way nature does as possible.

When bulbs are grown outdoors, fall and winter weather gives the cool, and then the cold, weather bulbs need. By the time winter is ready to turn into spring, the bulb's roots are well developed. Then, when the weather warms up a bit, the spring flowering bulbs start to grow and produce their beautiful flowers.

When the bulbs are grown indoors, you must supply first the cool, then the cold, and finally the warm weather the bulbs need. Here's what you have to do to grow hardy bulbs like tulips, snowdrops, oxalis, amaryllis, and bluebells indoors.

First, buy the largest bulbs you can afford. Usually they are called forcing size. When you get the bulbs home, keep them in a cool (about 50°), airy spot. If they are packed in boxes or bags, open them up and spread them out.

When you are ready to plant them, select a large, stubby-shaped red clay pot. There are special bulb forcing pots and these are best for the job. Cover the drainage hole in the pot with a piece of broken clay pot or with a piece of wire mesh. Either one will keep the soil from pouring out the drainage hole. Fill the pot about half full with a regular potting soil mixture that has a little extra sand added. Push your nice, large bulbs into the soil mixture, but be certain you push the bulbs in with the flat end down. Put in enough bulbs so they are quite close together, but do not touch each other or touch the sides of the pot. Then cover with another inch of soil so about three-quarters of an inch of the bulb top still shows out. Carefully water the soil and put the pot into your refrigerator. That's right . . . into the refrigerator for the bulbs' cooling off period. For a school project, you can force bulbs for blooming indoors on a larger scale. Make up many pots of bulbs, and instead of putting them into the refrigerator for cooling, put them into a cold basement, unheated garage, or into the ground, pot and all. If some land is available, dig a hole or trench, put in the pots filled with bulbs, cover with six to ten inches of sand or peat moss, and wait for the time you want to force the bulbs into bloom.

Allow the potted bulbs to stay in the cold at least ten weeks to develop strong, healthy root systems. Then bring the pots inside and keep them in a cool, dark spot for another two weeks. After sprouts appear and are about two or three inches tall, water the plants and move them out into the sunlight. Then treat these wonderful plants like you would any other indoor plants. Watch and water them so they never dry out. Give the pots a quarter turn each day so the flower stalks do not bend too much toward the sun. When the flower heads become big and heavy, stake them upright. Do all this and you

*Forcing bulbs indoors produces an array of colorful blooms: tulips (left), oxalis, and bluebells. The diagram on the right shows how the bulb pots should be planted.*

will have wonderful flowers to enjoy during the nastiest parts of the winter and spring.

There are several other ways you can force bulbs into bloom indoors, but the best and perhaps most exciting is called water forcing. For this kind of forcing you don't use soil, only water for certain bulbs and water and pebbles for others.

Try water alone for forcing hyacinths. You can either use the special hyacinth glass (shaped like an hourglass — bulb goes on top, water on bottom, and roots grow into bottom) or any narrow glass that will hold the bulb in the proper position — flat side down. Fill the glass with water until it almost reaches the bottom of the hyacinth bulb. Drop a small piece of charcoal into the water to keep it clear. Put the glass with the bulb in position into a cool, dark place. The temperature should not rise above 50° while the roots are forming.

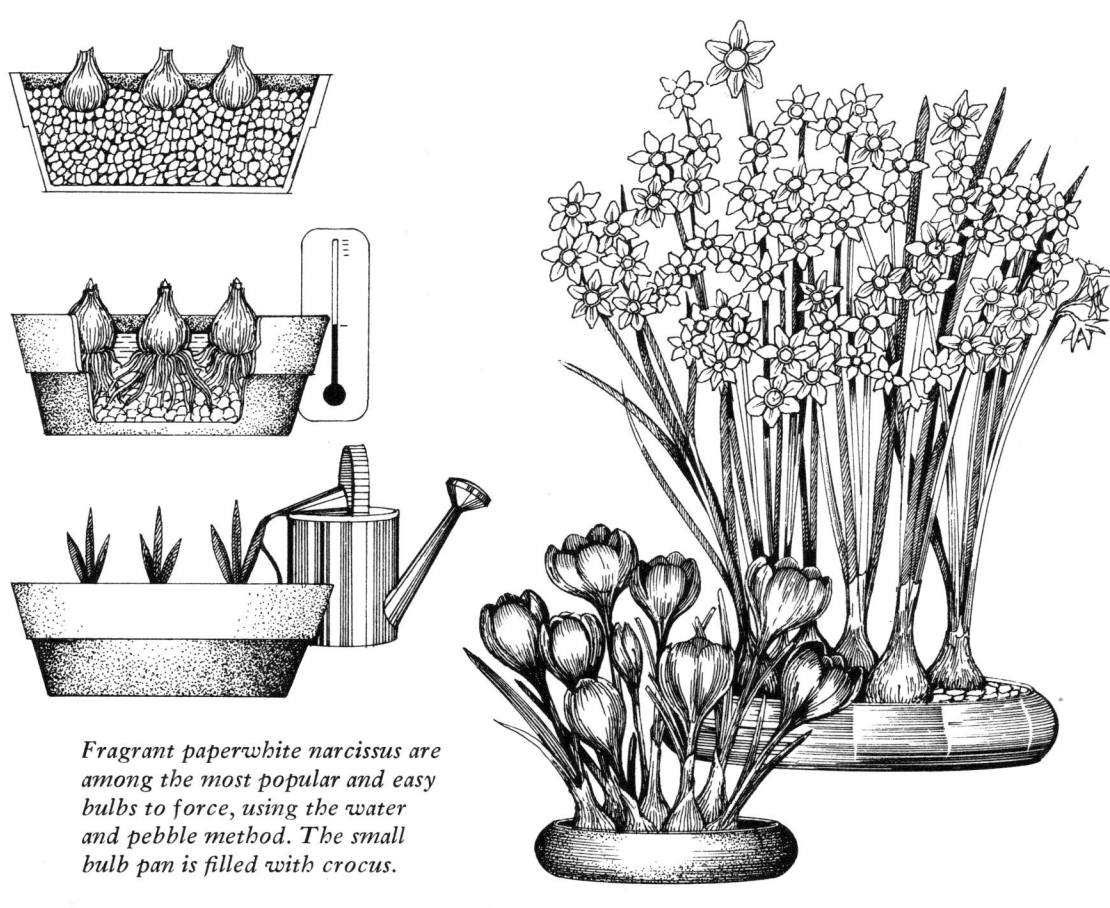

*Fragrant paperwhite narcissus are among the most popular and easy bulbs to force, using the water and pebble method. The small bulb pan is filled with crocus.*

When the stubby flower buds appear and the roots come out of the bottom of the bulb and are at least three inches long, move the glass into a spot that is a little warmer (53° to 57°) and in the light. Do not move the glass into the sunlight, just out of the dark. When the shoots are about six inches long and a healthy green color, bring them out into the open, into full light. After the flowers have burst into beautiful bloom, they will stay pretty longer if you keep the temperature at 60° to 65°.

Paperwhite narcissus, crocus, colchicums, and the bridal favorite, lily-of-the-valley, can be forced into bloom using the water and pebbles method. All you need do is put about two inches of pebbles, sand, marble chips, or gravel into a flat pan that will hold water (no drainage hole). Push the bulbs, flat side down into the pebbles. Be sure they are in tight and will not topple over. Just like the ones forced in soil, the bulbs should be close to each other but not touching each other or the sides of the pan. Add more pebbles all around the bulbs so only the top half of each bulb can be seen above the pebbles. Hold the bulb top steady with your fingers as you pack the pebbles all around the bulb.

Drop a few pieces of washed aquarium filter charcoal into the pan and add water. Pour the water carefully into the pan until it reaches the bottom of the bulbs. Stop as soon as it does. Do not add so much water that it reaches above the level of the pebbles or stones.

Put the pan into a dark cool spot for two to three weeks so the roots get a chance to grow. Check the bulbs every day and add water as necessary to keep the water in the pan at the same level it was when you started. When the roots have grown, put the pan onto a sunny, warm windowsill and watch for the flowers. In a few weeks you'll have some of the prettiest flowers you have ever seen.

If you can get the timing right, you can add these wonderful bulb flowers to your list of indoor plants that are very special and very easy to grow.

# Cacti and Succulents

How long could you go without a drink of water? Scientists say a person would last about four weeks without water. A cactus plant can live over twenty years without a single drink of water. That tells us a lot about how cacti and succulents grow and how we should take care of them.

Cacti and succulents are plants that store water in their fleshy leaves or stems so they do not have to depend on rainfall. Most of the cacti come from desert areas where there is no rain for long periods of time. Another kind of cactus comes from the jungle and is as different in looks and requirements from the desert cactus as can be.

There are thousands and thousands of different cacti, many of which have armor-hard leaves and stems, interesting shapes and sizes, and lots and lots of thorns. They are very easy and enjoyable to grow, if you remember they are not like most other plants. They do not need nearly the same amount of water as most other plants.

To grow desert cacti in your home you need a place that gets about six hours of direct sunlight every day, clay pots, and sandy soil. When you first get your cacti home, keep them out of the sunlight but still in bright light. Slowly give the plants more and more sunlight until they are getting up to about six hours each day.

Unlike other plants that do well in most kinds of pots, cacti do well only in pots that do not hold water. Be certain you use a pot with a drainage hole. Do not use a plastic or a glazed pot that has no drainage hole. If the pot holds moisture, the roots will rot and your cactus will die. Unglazed clay pots with drainage holes are usually the best ones for cacti.

The soil, too, has to be special for cacti. A regular potting soil mix will be much too "heavy" for cacti, so you can either add a lot of sand to a regular mix or you can buy special cactus potting soil mixes, ready-made at your local garden shop.

After your cacti have completed their growing season, the best thing you can do for them is — nothing. During the fall and winter "store them away" in a cool spot (about 45°) without soil around their roots and no light and no water. As spring approaches, put them back into pots with their special cactus mix soil, add a little bit of water, and bring them out into the light. Give them more and more light so that when spring comes they are up to six hours of sunlight each day.

Some of the interestingly named cacti you should try:

    Old-man Cactus — *Cephalocereus senilis*
    Rat-tail Cactus — *Aporocactus flagelliformis*
    Old-lady Cactus — *Mammillaria*
    Prickly Pear — *Opuntia littoralis*
    Organ Pipe Cactus — *Lemaireocereus marginatus*
    Eagle Claws — *Echinocactus horizonthalonius*
    Rainbow Cactus — *Echinocereus dasyacanthus*

*Cacti come in many different varieties and shapes and some of them have exquisite blooms. Clockwise from the top: orchid cactus, Christmas cactus, rat-tail cactus, organ pipe cactus, and in the center, a prickly pear with fruit and flowers.*

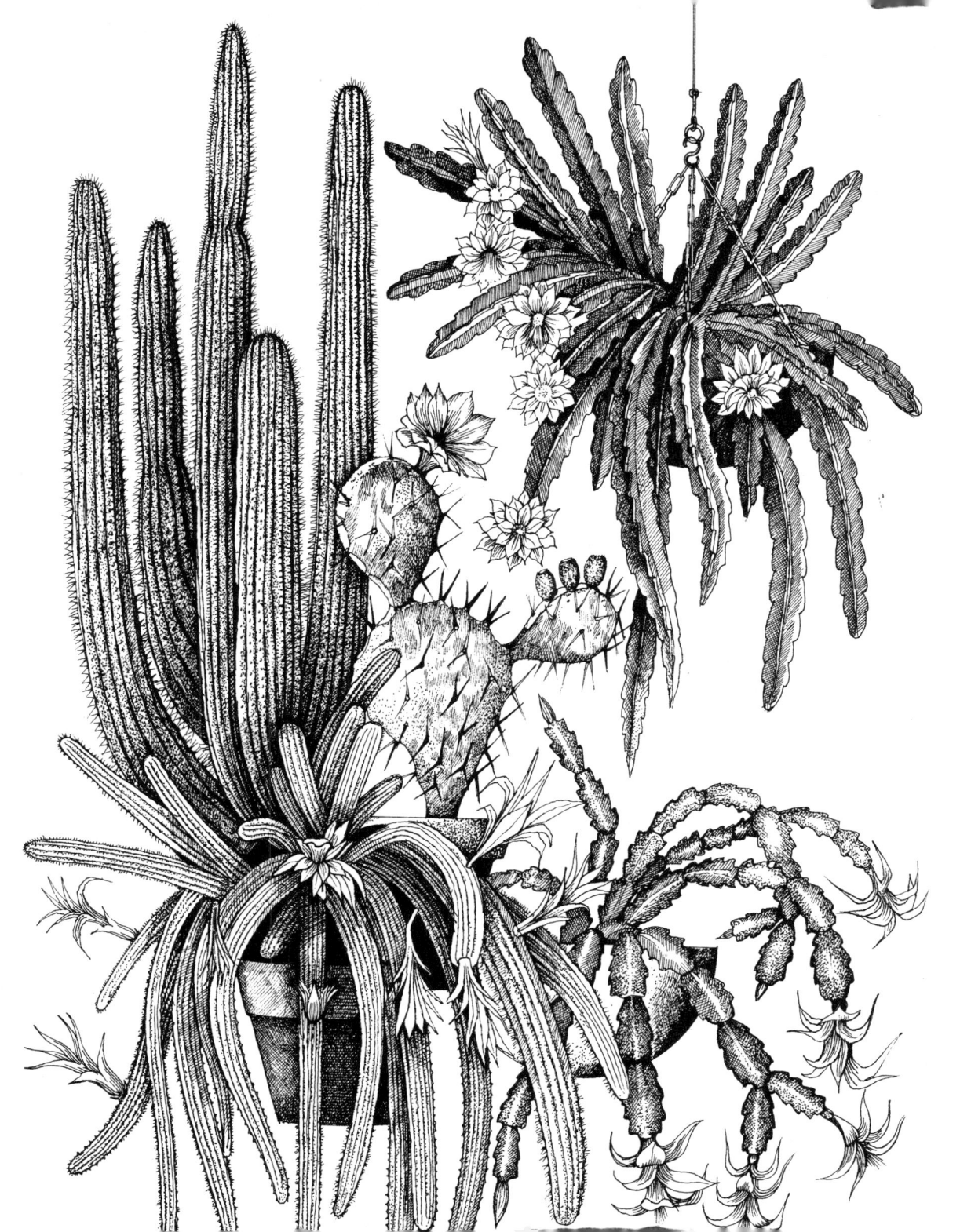

Although jungle cacti are quite different looking from desert cacti and require different care, they too are well worth trying. To get the best results from your jungle cacti you must make them feel at home. Pot them in a soil that is like the soil found in the climate in which they live naturally. Make sure the soil is rich and full of peat moss and humus. Give these plants more water than you give desert cacti but less than you give "regular" plants. Keep them out of direct sunlight, but give them plenty of bright light. Here are some of the special jungle cacti you should try:

Orchid Cactus — *Epiphyllum oxypetalum*
Mistletoe Cactus — *Rhipsalis burchelli*
Christmas Cactus — *Schlumbergera bridgesii*
Thanksgiving Cactus — *Zygocactus*

*Several kinds of succulents combine well in a dish garden. Here are a little stone face, a prickly crown of thorns, and a jade plant with thick, water-storing leaves.*

There are so many different plants in the succulent group (succulents have thick, water-storing leaves and stems to help them survive droughts) it would take a whole book or two to describe how they grow. Instead, here are some you should try, but only after you find out from your nurseryman how to care for these plants. Remember, they are different from other plants, so check before you buy:

      Burro's Tail — *Sedum*
      Cone Plant — *Conophytum globosum*
      Air Plant — *Kalanchoe pinnata*
      Jade Plant — *Crassula argentea*
      Crown of Thorns — *Euphorbia splendens*
      Stone Face — *Lithops olivalea*

# Gift Plants

Many of us give and receive gift plants during the various holiday seasons. These plants are greatly appreciated as gifts because they keep on giving for a long time. They have been raised by experts under perfect greenhouse conditions. When we get or give these specimen plants, they are beautiful and blooming. If they are neglected, they will last only a very short time. If they are cared for properly, they can keep on giving pleasure and cheer, sometimes for as long as several years.

Here are some plants often given as gifts at holiday time and how to care for them in your home. If you give or get plants not included here, be sure to ask a florist or a nurseryman to tell you the best way to keep them living and blooming.

*Azalea*

After a few days of enjoying your azalea just as it comes from the florist, remove all foil and ribbons. Be sure the drainage hole is not blocked by tinfoil wrapping or anything else. Then follow the growing suggestions listed for these flowering plants on page 10.

### *Capsicum* (Red Pepper Plant)

These plants make wonderful gifts because they give a double reward — flowers in the spring and colorful fruit in the fall. Grown from seed, these plants have lots of tiny fruits that look like peppers around Christmastime.

Grow these on the cool side because too much warmth causes the fruit and the leaves to drop. Give the plants full sun and water regularly and you will have pretty, decorative plants for the holidays.

### *Cyclamen* (Shooting Star)

Keep these pretty plants cool at night and you can keep them blooming for many months. Always move the plants into areas where the overnight temperature is no higher than 50°-55°. Water the plants thoroughly, but do not let them get soggy or the roots will rot and the plant will die. Give them lots of light, but no direct, hot sunlight and the buds will keep coming and opening for a long time. See page 13 for more directions on how to care for and raise cyclamens.

### *Euphorbia Pulcherrima* (Poinsettia)

Start your "saving" program for your poinsettia as soon as possible. Keep the plants warm during the day (70°) and cool (55°) at night. Water lightly. Too much water and the lower leaves will start to fall.

After the flowers fade, use less and less water, for the soil should be kept on the dry side. Repot in the spring in soil that is rich in peat moss and humus. Give lots of sun and water regularly. Pinch back the tops of the plant so it stays compact and bushy, but stop pinching early in August. Fertilize with liquid organic fertilizer all during the summer growth period.

*Both these plants, the poinsettia with its showy red flowers (left) and the red pepper plant with its bright fruit, are at their most decorative in December.*

Poinsettias bloom only when there are less than twelve hours of light each day. Put your plants into a dark closet after sunset each evening. When the colored flower bracts appear, you can leave plants out at night, but the biggest flowers come when the plant gets a regular amount of darkness at night.

*Schlumbergera Bridgesii* (Christmas Cactus)

Beautiful hanging blooms at Christmastime are the feature of this succulent plant. Unlike others of the group, this plant needs lots of moisture during the growing season. When it has finished growing, keep it quite dry. Give it a lot of sunlight and normal house temperatures, a little on the cool side both during the daytime and at night. Treat it exactly as you would treat the poinsettia (page 51) by giving it total darkness from 5:00 P.M. to 8:00 A.M. in the fall and until buds start to form.

*Solanum Pseudocapsicum* (Jerusalem Cherry)

Very popular around Christmastime because of their bright red fruit, these decorative plants do best if kept cool. They have been grown

*The decorative Jerusalem cherry is a popular gift plant for Christmas.*

in cool greenhouses, so give them the cool treatment in your home. Give them a lot of sunlight and water only when the soil dries out and you will have a pretty, colorful plant for a long time.

# Indoor Garden Pests

Wherever there are plants there will be insects. Some plants attract more insects than others, but almost all plants attract some insects and can be bothered by certain diseases. How do you get rid of insects that chew on leaves, suck out juices, and generally make a mess of many plants? How do you fight diseases that hurt and even kill your plants? Better yet, how do you keep these pests and diseases from coming in the first place?

One of the best ways to keep your plants healthy and free of pests is to practice good gardening. First, select plants you know resist certain diseases. The places where you buy plants can tell you this. Then be certain you give your plants enough food and water, but not too much. Overfeeding and overwatering can cause as much trouble as starving the plants. Next, be sure you keep your plants and the places they grow as clean as possible.

One way to protect your plants from hungry insects is to spray them with natural bug repellents. For example, many bugs hate the smell of garlic and onions. So, mash up some garlic, onion, or both, then put the paste into a jar of water and let it stand overnight. Spray this liquid on your plants and many bugs will stay far, far away. Other things you can use for sprays are hot pepper, cayenne pepper, a little salt in water, and even some soapy (natural soap, not detergent) dishwater. You can also sprinkle some dry black pepper on your plants and it will keep bugs away. Give your plants a shower in the bathtub or kitchen sink and you will knock the bugs off your plants. But remember, before you put the plant under the shower spray, cover the soil with an aluminum foil collar, then gently spray away. A common houseplant pest, mealybug, can be picked off with a cotton swab dipped in alcohol.

As a last resort, and that is what it should be, you can always fall back on chemical insecticides in aerosol cans. If you must use these sprays, use them sparingly and exactly as the directions indicate. Check with your local garden shop and have them help you select the safest chemicals to do the job. But if there is any way you can avoid using man-made chemicals, such as by using the natural methods just described, stick with nature's way.

Whichever method you select, know what you are doing and what you are fighting. Many fine books are available to help you identify insects and diseases that attack plants. Check back and forth between books and plants so you are certain you are fighting the insect you think you are fighting.

# Other Books to Read

Abraham, George. *The Green Thumb Book of Indoor Gardening*. Englewood Cliffs, N.J.: Prentice-Hall, 1967.

Ballard, Ernesta D. *Garden in Your House* (rev. ed.). New York: Harper and Row, 1971.

Brooklyn Botanic Garden Record. *Plants and Gardens*. Baltimore: Brooklyn Botanic Garden, 1972.

———. *A House Plant Primer*. Baltimore: Brooklyn Botanic Garden, 1972.

Crockett, James U. and the Editors of Time-Life Books. *Flowering House Plants*. New York: Time-Life Books, 1972.

———. *Foliage House Plants*. New York: Time-Life Books, 1972.
New York: Time-Life Books, 1972.

Faust, Joan Lee. *The New York Times Book of House Plants*. New York: Quadrangle Books, 1973.

Fenten, D. X. *Gardening...Naturally*. New York: Franklin Watts, Inc., 1973.

———. *Plants for Pots*. Philadelphia: J. B. Lippincott, 1969.

Fitch, Charles M. *The Complete Book of Houseplants*. New York: Hawthorn Books, 1972.

Kramer, Jack. *1000 Beautiful House Plants and How to Grow Them*. New York: William Morrow, 1969.

McDonald, Elvin. *The World Book of House Plants*. New York: Popular Library, 1972.

# Index

Abutilon, 10
Acinetta Orchids, 19
Aeschynanthus Parvifolus, 10
African Violets, 4, 20, 35
Aglaonema, 23
Air Plant, 49
Amaryllis, 40
Araucaria, 23
Aspidistra, 23-24
Azalea, 10-11, 50

Basket vines, 10
Begonia, 11
Beloperone, 12
Bluebells, 40
Bottom watering, 4-5
Bougainvillea, 12
Brassavola Orchids, 19
Bromeliads, 24
Bug repellents, 55-56
Bulbs, 40-44
Burro's Tail, 49

Cabbage, 34
Cacti, 45-49
    Desert, 45-47
    Jungle, 47-49
Cacti mix, 7
Calamondin Orange, 31
Calathea, 24
Calceolaria, 12-13
Capsicum, 51
Carrot, 34
Cast-Iron Plant, 23
Cattleya Orchids, 19
Chinese Evergreen, 23
Christmas Cactus, 48-53
Cineraria, 21
Citrus, 31-34
    Limonia, 31
    Mitus, 31
    Taitensis, 31
Colchicum, 44
Coleus, 26
Cone Plant, 49

Containers, 8
Corn, 34
Corn Plant, 27
Crassula Argentea, 49
Crocus, 44
Crossandra, 13
Croton, 26
Crown of Thorns, 49
Cyclamen, 13-14, 51
Cycnoches Orchids, 19

Desert Cacti, 45-47
Dieffenbachia, 26-27
Dish garden, 36-39
Dracena, 27
Drainage, 8
Dumb Cane, 26-27
Dwarf Citrus, 32-33
Dwarf Peaches, 34
Dwarf Pears, 34
Dwarf Plum, 34
Dwarf Vegetables, 34

Eagle Claws Cactus, 46
English Ivy, 29
Epidendrum Orchids, 19
Euphorbia Pulcherrima, 51-52
Euphorbia Splendens, 49

Fertilizer, 7-8
    organic, 7-8
    water soluble, 7-8
Ficus, 27
Fiddle Leaf Fig, 27
Flowering Maple, 10
Flowering plant mix, 7
Flowering plants, 9-21
Foliage plant mix, 7
Foliage Plants, 22-30
Forcing, 40-44
    water, 42-44

Fuchsia, 4, 15

Garden pests, 55-56
Gas, 5
Geranium, 4, 19-12
    Carefree, 20
    Dwarf, 20
    Fancy Leaf, 20
    Ivy Leaf, 20
    Martha Washington, 20
    Zonal, 20
Gift plants, 50-54
Gloxinia, 4, 15
Gynura, 27-28

Hedera, 29
Herbs, 34
Hibiscus, 15-16
Houseplant mix, 7
Humidity, 5
Hyacinth, 43-44

Impatiens, 17-18
Indian Rubber Tree, 27
Indoor foods, 31-34
Insecticides, 56
Ivy, 29

Jade Plant, 49
Jerusalem Cherry, 53-54
Jungle Cacti, 47-49

Kalanchoe, 18
Kalanchoe Pinnati, 49

Lady's Eardrops, 15
Lantana, 18
Lettuce, 34
Light, 2-4
Lily-of-the-Valley, 44
Lipstick Plant, 10

Lithops Olivalea, 49

Maranta, 24
Mealybug, 56
Mexican Flame Vine, 21
Miniature plants, 35-39
Mistletoe Cactus, 48

Nagami Kumquat, 34
Norfolk Island Pine, 23

Odontoglossum Orchids, 19
Old-Lady Cactus, 46
Old-Man Cactus, 46
Oncidium Orchids, 19
Orchid Cactus, 48
Orchids, 19
    Epiphytic, 19
    Terrestrial, 19
Organ Pipe Cactus, 46
Organic fertilizer, 7-8
Otaheite Orange, 31
Oxalis, 40

Paper-Flower, 12
Paperwhite Narcissus, 44
Paphiopedilum Orchids, 19
Parlor Ivy, 21
Passiflora, 19
Passionflower, 4, 19
Patience Plant, 17-18
Pelargonium, 19-20
    Carefree, 20
    Dwarf, 20
    Fancy Leaf, 20
    Ivy Leaf, 20
    Martha Washington, 20
    Zonal, 20
Peperomia, 29
Persian Lime, 34

Phalaenopsis Orchids, 19
Philodendron, 29-30
Pineapple, 24
Pocketbook Plant, 12-13
Poinsettia, 51-52
Pollination, 33-34
Pomegranate, 34
Ponderosa Lemon, 31
Pots, 8
Pouch Flower, 12-13
Prayer Plant, 24
Prickly Pear, 46

Rainbow Cactus, 46
Rat-Tail Cactus, 46
Red Pepper Plant, 51
Rex Begonias, 11
Rose of China, 15-16
Rubber Plant, 27

Saintpaulia, 20
Sansevieria, 30
Schlumbergera Bridgesii, 53
Sedum, 49
Senecio, 21
Shooting Star, 13-15, 51
Shrimp Plant, 12
Snake Plant, 30
Snowdrops, 40
Soil, 7
Solanum Pseudocapsicum, 53-54
Stanhopea Orchids, 19
Stone Face, 49
Succulents, 45-49

Temperature, 6-7
Terrarium, 36-39
Thanksgiving Cactus, 48
Tomato, 34
Tulips, 40

Vanda Orchids, 19
Velvet Plant, 27-28
Ventilation, 5

Water, 4-5

Water forcing, 42-44
Water soluble fertilizer, 7-8
Wax Begonias, 11

Zygocactus, 48

# About the Author

D. X. Fenten began gardening as a weekend project in his Long Island backyard. His hobby led to a garden filled with flowers, fruits, and vegetables, a house filled with thriving indoor plants, and the writing of a number of books on gardening.

His first children's book was *Plants for Pots: Projects for Indoor Gardeners* and he has written *Gardening...Naturally*, an introduction to organic gardening, and *Natural Foods: A Concise Guide* for Franklin Watts, Inc. He is also the author of gardening and photography books for adults and career guidance books for young people.

Mr. Fenten was born and grew up in New York City and has B.A. and M.A. degrees from New York University. He teaches writing and cinematography to high school students. He lives in Greenlawn, New York with his wife Barbara, co-author of *Natural Foods*, and their two children, Donna and Jeff.

# About the Artist

Howard Berelson was born in Brooklyn, New York, attended Pratt Institute there, and now makes his home in Brooklyn. He has illustrated several children's books, including *Gardening...Naturally* and *Natural Foods,* and is a sculptor.